RED GLOVES

Rebecca Watts was born in Suffolk in 1983
and currently lives in Cambridge. Her debut
poetry collection, *The Met Office Advises
Caution*, was published by Carcanet in 2016.
She is also the editor of *Elizabeth Jennings:
New Selected Poems* (Carcanet, 2019).

Also by Rebecca Watts, from Carcanet

REBECCA WATTS

Red Gloves

CARCANET

First published in Great Britain in 2020 by
Carcanet
Alliance House, 30 Cross Street
Manchester M2 7AQ
www.carcanet.co.uk

A CIP catalogue record for this book is
available from the British Library.

ISBN 978 1 78410 955 4

Book design by Andrew Latimer
Printed in Great Britain by SRP Ltd, Exeter, Devon

The publisher acknowledges financial
assistance from Arts Council England.

CONTENTS

RED GLOVES

ECONOMICS

Everything comes down to numbers in the end.

This morning a blackbird woke me up; five swans in formation
trailed their silver chevrons upriver, unbothered by
the heron's slow torpedo; three horses in maroon jackets stood
mystified by their own breath. A greenfinch and thirty-nine
cows patterned the field; twin black labs trotted through
the long grass, jingling, and unearthed a compact of magpies.
I didn't count the dandelion clocks, there were so many.

You ask me would I move to the city to be with you.
I'm telling you what I saw; you can do the maths.

DEFINITIONS

Husband
a strong word   money
if he gives it   security
if he's there   someone
to hold the baby   when you ask

Friend
a lame word   the crow
who shows up without asking
who empties the washing machine
while you cry yourself to sleep
who lines up your socks in pairs
on the radiator   so it's easier
to bundle them away when they're dry

Lover
a word not spoken   dealer
in tongues   hands
eyes   arms

RED GLOVES

The women are carrying the coffin. Under the fear
of slippage they make slow steps.
We cannot say that they advance.

More than one woman is weathering – from the cool
top of her head to her strained fingers to her toes
pushed together in interview shoes – the urge,
like a rip tide, to run backwards and away.
Today is not a normal day.

How awkward we are.
Even were they to confer it would not be possible
for these four women to set down their load
with elegance. The military could manage it –
but military is system, control from above.

The women are moving from within.
More than one will go to ground today.
More than one will be tugged
otherwards. Husbands and children.
How requiring, how embarrassable we are.

One is wearing red woollen gloves. She is pressing them
to the wicker as though without her hands' small force
the entire construction would fold.

AMNESIAC

Rush of the waves in your ear
you wake, begin
each day. Beach stones

shuffle and fall, shift
to accommodate your tread,
shuffle again.

No trace of you left.
Wind-pawed
you stand at the edge,

salt crystals
fizzing round your toes,
skin pinking

as the North
Sea slaps then
smothers you,

taking as it finds.
Swimmer,

when you breathe again
there's no such thing
as cold, only

the water's grip
anchoring, slipping
as you kick against it.

MUSIC IN FOUR PARTS

i. m. Fergal O'Mahony

Once there was a box
and the box was carved with an intricate pattern
inlayed with mother of pearl
and the lid was fastened with a silver clasp
which shone when lamplight struck it
and when the lid was lifted
there was music.

*

Fingers
defying vision, drilled until such
freedom comes that the eyes read
sound and the brain is rapt in precision's
blur and the present is
nothing but the dear, dear air
beneath two palms.

*

There is a scale
for everything.
There is up and
there is down
and if you play with both hands
you can be up and down
in the same moment.

*

A metronome stopped
is a loudness.
The crowd, which doesn't know
it is a crowd, holds on
to the outbreath, waits
for the tock   tock   tock
to resume the necessary music.

you'll be inclined
to regret the body: its readiness
to spoil the good
clean
margin with a living stain.
You'll resist the fact you can't at all times
contain
the clever business
of circulation: that occasionally a press-
ure builds and has to be released,
or the skin's defence is breached
so a little of your mess
leaks
out. You'll sigh,
acknowledging that the printed word's
no shield against the givens:
seep-
age, decay.
You'll read
on, distracted by
the rust/blot/smear and the question
of whether you'll be forced to pay.

SALVATION

Isn't it glorious! said Maria
when I caught up with her beside the river
on a 15°C December morning
in brilliant sunshine.

Let's enjoy it!
Before the water's risen to our knees
the Dutch will have invented
something wonderful.

SWEET PEAS FOR THE WEDDING

glorify even as they
fall away

defy
all sceptics
all resisters

folding in over out
purple pink white

luxuriant
coy and complete-
ly at home

open to anything

head's weight
and heart's weightlessness

balanced
for a day

three days at most
once you cut them

softening
as they droop

and you look
not wanting to touch

WORSHIP NOT THE OBJECT BUT THE THING IT REPRESENTS

Apprentice

Who is it I love? I gaze through layers
at The Virgin Mother and The Infant Christ,
but here's *our* Mary with her child wrapped
in silks (Egyptian blue, verdigris), and
tiny boats all busy on the sea behind
them. And then in her eyes (burnt umber,
yielding as clay) there's Maria, who hardly
moved the whole time we drew, and never
complained, but soothed and shushed and dandled
the baby so it smiled for us again.

Novice

The trouble is the doll – so hard and so
unnaturally shiny! *Here is a
focus for your love of Christ*, they said, *to
practise your devotion on*. But its knees don't
bend and its stuck face smells like a workshop.
Once I saw a statue of the Christ child,
his chubby legs rendered so soft you could
pinch them. And in the paintings his skin's as
kissable as a peach. Like love made flesh.
It's fine here but I miss my family.

Scholar

Yet they come, like bailiffs, with their roll
and index, their hammers for the printer's
plates and their buckets of fire. To purge
a man of sinful thoughts, burn paper?
An idea is already smoke; it crosses
channels, regardless of ink. And
freedom is the stuff of days: men's minds
cleave to it as monks to a rosary.
Poor faithful puppets: they knock and knock.
I memorise the contents of my books.

SURVEILLANCE

The neighbours have gone away

All day
and all night
the light conducts its inquiry

                                    no

its interrogation

The professor striding towards the meadow
trailing a gold spaniel
is interrogated

The boy dragging a big stick
along the road to dinnertime
is interrogated

as are the couple winding up
their argument before the corner
(they may resume it later)

                    *

For a week the light trains its message
on an unwild garden
a narrow street
                            and me

Leaf shapes conspire
on the wall above the mirror
while we try to stay asleep

Dawn's stealth is obliterated
but the light has its directive

The pauses in the blackbird's song
are his attempts to swallow it

A HISTORY OF MINOR CONFLICT

Her aim is to acquire their arguments –
replay each one slowly enough that
she can visualise the words as script,
which she will type, print off and file,
documenting the processes of failure

precisely. The collection will require a strong room.
It will take up space – but not as shouting
people do, absorbing all the air, making it hard
to breathe. Boxes, folders, paper, ink:
a level silence. Orderly (she thinks)

and true – the past, defined as if it mattered,
a cache of lines no one's about to speak,
persons once inclined to listen moved on.

WHEN I WAS A GIRL

I was a boy
in my dad's flat cap
and my mum's old painting shirt
and my brother's outgrown trousers
and my granddad's braces

and I sang nice and loud
and I danced in bare feet
and pretending and dirt
were no bother to me

and now I'm a woman
I covet expensive tailoring
in the workhouse style
feeling most at home
in the get-up of an orphan in a fiction

BUILDING

In rooms the students talk as though
keying return
means
frag
men
tation

as though everything about us
is prose
till someone comes along and
chops /
us /
up //

(oh Eliot
in this you did not
          help us!)

Look here:

                              nothing until I
                              go and point it

                              walls of white bricks
                              we can't see to knock on
                              except in relief

                              these dark lines
                              mortar

ENCORE

Will the blackbird be homeless now the buddleia
in which he nested and sang
sweet spring is hacked?

Will the wall be a wall now the shambling
rose, which lent its yellow lights,
has been cut back?

Veins of old ivy, like Lichtenberg figures, cling
to the brickwork. Lichen's soft language
spreads in the joins. Something

new is wobbling outwards from the trellis. The he-
bird makes of gutter-pipe and shed roof
a singing-post.

NOTATIONS FOR A HOSPITAL

for Addenbrooke's Arts

Level 10: a crow
flirts with the guardrail. Blue sky,
inky flutterings.

*

Descend, walk headlong
into heath, all grass blazing.
Fingertips brush sedge.

*

A chair abandoned
in an unlit stairwell might
be art. Say something.

*

These corridors self-
refer. Rosemary for re-
membrance. Love's bluebells.

CORRIDOR

Archives bring us closer
to the nub
of the matter –

put flesh on
the past – cherish
those instruments designed

to mend us, which
hung in their display
case look like weapons.

ADMISSION

What am I afraid of?
The breaching of skin.
Violation of laws that
separate outside from in.
Liquidation of the thing
I call me. Or perhaps
solidity: my body
no more special than
that vase in which roses,
little pink fists, bloom.

WHEN ALL THIS IS OVER

I mean to run fast

where the buzz of machines
and the humdrum of walls
and the flummox of words
are behind me

where no one not even
myself observes me

oh yes I intend
to run in the dark

where the thud of the feet eclipses
the thud of the heart

where a chill night bites me
and a slick sweat coats me
and streetlamps gild me
and church bells ring me

GRASMERE EARLY

After the edginess
      of flint

it's pure
         silk

          the lake
slipping its skin

     mutual acclimatisation

first arms
      then shoulders
acquiring an antique tinge

ale through a glass
            grip
     so tight you forget
who's cooling who

eyes widening
to take it in

       felled utterly
as you swim an
almost perfect circle

AT THE SANCTUARY

Coal embers
are the eyes of the eagle
which burn through the wires
                  and burn
through the children who point
to the pellet of mouse gunk on the gravel
oblivious of their erasure

from the world as seen
in the eyes of the eagle
which burn through time and age
                  the invisible cage
and give shape   sharp   bodily
to the lure of no mind: a Zen
Buddhist on a rock in a high place

GLOUCESTER, MASSACHUSETTS

I.

The man who designed these houses
didn't know fishermen.
He confused the ocean with a view.

Upstairs, where she paces,
the floorboards could show her a face –
its worry lines, its ringed eyes.

Often there's a speck,
a blip in the haze of horizon,
a shimmer at the edge of vision.

When she tears herself away
she sees windows in everything.
And the unreformable sea.

2.

They knew
the fisherman's theory of colour –
how the spectrum is a myth –

there is no continuum,
only a saltatory progression
from this to this to that.

White is still close to the surface,
in touch with the thunderous
sky with its load of oxygen.

Green is the body of the wave,
solid and roomy
as the earth they couldn't love.

And black –
black is the submarine's domain
from which no fishing boat

is coming back.

MATRIMONY

early road	sombre light
may I	would you
thanks	continue

INTERNS

Five days out of seven we go to the Work Room. We work on Projects.
We turn on the computers cheerfully and tap the keys. We exchange stories
but not about our Projects, to which we've been specially, individually
    assigned. Now and then
He descends and, rather than gliding from the building to unspecified,
    important places,
enters the Work Room like a blast of liquid nitrogen, only talking. We tap
    cryogenically
in time to a collective, unvoiced *Don't pick me*. Whomever He picks,
we all listen to the Brief with our best listening – as a rabbit
sluiced in 1200 lumens of lorry light on shuddering tarmac might be said to
    be listening.
When He exits the air unpresses itself from the ceiling and slowly expands
    until it once again touches all seventeen corners of the Work Room,
where we tap the keys cheerfully, grateful for the opportunity.

GLAMOUR

Life isn't glamorous

for the hawk employed to circle landfill –

deterring the scavengers that flock here
to feed and nest in the nearby villages.

For us, released from the office, this
frenzy of birdlife in the midst of
dystopia is spectacular: against
the rubbish's mishmashed colour
and the lazy sky

               clarity of white and black –

seagulls and crows.

                    We see it by chance,
          the hawk
patient on its perch
while a handler squirts disinfectant from a plastic bottle
all over it,
drenching its feathers,
disabling it from flight.

                    We look
and see beauty in its bedragglement,
trust,

                    as it waits, growing dry
amid concrete and dumper trucks.

THE STUDIO

little lady little man
little pot little pan
little table little chair
little cupboard little stair
little plant little leaves
little rooftop little eaves
little cake little pie
little naptime lullaby
little blanket little book
little corner little nook
little cushion little frame
little thing without a name
little statue little bell
little bauble little shell
little lamp little pin
little box to put it in
little apron little jug
little window little rug
little postcard little rock
little candle little clock
little broom little door
little greedy wanting more

FORCES FALLS

As we leaned
into the hill,
nudging toeholds,
clutching at ferns,
trying not to brush
bare legs against bracken
(ticks live inside bracken)

with our swimming stuff
shoved down the backs
of our shorts
(having left your daughter
on an outcrop with the others and
only some ants
in the range of her interest)

and
edged
down, wary
of the slipperiness
of moss,
wary of
gravity

then, finding a flattish spot,
peeled off our boots and socks
(the ancient sponginess of moss!)
and wriggled into our bikinis
and crab-crawled over rocks
to lower ourselves
into the well beneath the falls,

Richard
was pointing his camera
at the sky, tracking
the shallow V of the golden eagle
sailing its eastern patch
(Haweswater to Rosgill
and the whole of the valley of Swindale)

which we missed,
because in that particular minute
all we sensed was a deep chill
(emptiness under our feet)
and all we saw was black water
and black walls
and neither of us thought to look up.

OH, SUSIE, IT IS DANGEROUS

Wisteria jabbing at the window – all that holds between you
this single sheet – thin pane – transparent border –
oh, Susie, do not open it – though it invites – though its scent
bewitches – do not lean across the table – do not let it in –
all Heaven – all Earth – these letters forming – all must be allowed
such Separation – degrees of Light – warm rays lying here –
cold papers pressed into a casket there – oh, Susie, hang the key
where None may reach – pale purple clusters – touch of the Eternal –
no doubt *soft* – oh, Susie, close your ears – to the tapping
as you breathe – imagine Snowfall – whitest Air –

IN THE POET'S BEDROOM

Oh look! She was real! Her dinky shoes!
A letter in the pocket of her pint-sized dress!

For $200 you can sit at her desk.
For an undisclosed sum you can try on her shoes

and try on her walk between opposite walls
(one two one two one two one two)

and gaze from her windows and stroke her wallpaper
and weep on her pillows and finger her shawls,

unchecked by self-consciousness as you do.
Such intimacies are yours by right.

Cite her as *Emily*, and feel that she might
(had she lived in your time) be enamoured of you.

SUNFLOWERS

Never bring inside what belongs outside.
Two days in, the meat-heads putrefy

and the studio thickens
with the seepage of plant matter and oils. Sweat

ripens the fibres of a shirt and the vision
contracts to permit only

yellow yellow
yellow (happy colour!)

and the big buds loom
and the brute stalks fester in the urn.

BARBECUES

In the future it'll be different, we can have barbecues –
you'll pop to Homebase for a new gas canister
and what the hell, splash out on a garden table
the lot of us can fit round (plastic but tasteful,
oval-shaped and forest-green, with six matching chairs)
and we'll arrive with a selection of salads in patterned bowls,
clingfilmed for freshness, and there'll be printed napkins
that won't blow away because it's perfectly still and warm,
the end of July, and the children'll sit on a blanket and
join the conversation and the laughter, and before we eat
we'll have a toast *To happy families*, and the meat'll be tender,
flavoursome but not charred, and when you lift the lid
to turn the sausages and see them bunched like
fingers in a boxer's mitt you'll feel only hunger and magically
won't recall the past in which I punched your daughter.

THE DESIRE PATH

Now I go back I notice

the jagged
fallen trees

and the new twigs I'd thought of as budding
bobbled with disease

and the birches'
unfocused eyes

and the scattering of feathers
like a planned demolition.

The river curls
round on itself. Someone

has knotted a scraggy
red ribbon

to a stick.
Soon the sleepy adder

will stir
under her quilt

and I am afraid
and ill-equipped to wade

the few metres that divide me
from the far bank

where spring is.

WHEREAS

(*a*) some of us develop the ability to love and be loved without distress
    – having seen reflected
in our mother's eyes an infant with a halo and pink cheeks it would be
    nigh on impossible
not to kiss (especially when sticky with tears); and having detected in
    our father's voice
that particular brand of ebullience that is the by-product of
    craftsmanship, when a man
knows he's made something perfect through an effort of which, at the
    time, he was only
semi-conscious; and not having been exposed to early bouts of
    separation from the source
of alleviation of physical and emotional suffering (the causes of which,
    at this stage in our development,
we lack the required powers of contemplation and reason to
    ascertain), such as (to give but one
example) being left to scream for hours in an old-fashioned pram on
    the other side of a sliding door;

(*b*) others of us, when grown, feel in relationships somewhat like a
    walnut, the stubborn
hard shell easily broken to reveal (as one might predict, based on the
    rattling sound moderate shaking
will produce) a contracted interior, preserved (one might say petrified)
    in a state of recoil
necessitated by the anxiety that accompanies anticipation of the
    sensation of touch
(even of contact with its frame, the very layer that protects it from the
    world) – so constricted,
in fact, that if it tightened any further it would wither to dust, leaving
    it vulnerable to dispersal

should any passer-by chance to exhale, dreamily or, indeed, with
    force, in its vicinity;
and as repair becomes impossible once the constituent parts have
    been scattered on the wind,

some of us are destined to fly apart without trace, while others of
    us may channel our lack
so that it carries us, gregarious, through an objectively charmed
    life, culminating in a family,
whose members will present, when subjected to analysis, as either
    (*a*) or (*b*).

FINDS

I could say: dragon's tooth,
philosopher's stone,
gold dust

but I'm clearing out the car on trade-in day

so I say: black toggle off your duffle coat,
pebble (I forget where from),
thin covering of sand.

But, but... says a tape I've never listened to,
which predates me and is labelled in your
earnest hand: BLUEPRINTS / NIGHT.

BE CAREFUL ON THE COBB

Be careful on the Cobb. High winds do not distinguish
man from dog, or mislaid crabbing bucket from discarded
chip fork. High winds will seize anything that's not tied down
and the Cobb will disown what isn't its to give.

Do not dip your toe, oh hasten away
from the barricade's edge, for the water's cold
and the currents that suck and churn and raise white
spirits and grey ghouls below the Cobb are keen.

And do not sit long on the prickly wall
with a canvas expression and paint-tube eyes.
Where the land drops off, disaster lies; our defences
are licked by a savage tongue,
and everything of use to us ends at the Cobb.

GRATITUDE

for the tremendous luck that's shepherded us here and now – without
which Billy (facing the wrong way, an impossible journey) and
Leo (heart rate decreasing, cord tightening around his neck)
wouldn't have made it to their names, and my friends,
terrified or brave, would be left (their innermost
secrets saturating the linen) with the rough
knowledge that to live we must push
blindly such bundles of hope
as we have towards
the future.

THE DRAWING ROOM

Another lovely, dark-green papered wall –
camellia-patterned, ferned and leafed –
has been spoiled by having to bear
portraits of gilded men. Oh, they
were famous, or

they weren't, and my sneeze
is a complex
amalgam of reverence
and allergy.
They lived; were painted; died,

and now I'd like to read my book
without them being there. I'd like to stare
at a lovely, dark-green papered wall and say
to nobody: camellia, fern, leaf.

ANCESTRY.COM

Here's what you invest in:
names; occupations; the places

(not worth visiting) of births, deaths and marriages.
You might as well fabricate

as you please: stories part
tedium, part logic, part modest

thrill. Your predictable reactions, the lines
neatly ploughed between

your eyebrows when you concentrate
should work to remind you

you've paid already. Look:
you're paying now.

MY BLUE PERIOD

No one could create great works
in those pyjamas, you said.

It's high time you got up
and got out, you said.

I'd love to tell you how
I did get out

        as out as out could be

               with all my clothes off

    walking away from this

           too too solid ground

the very minute the sea

       melted over that groyne

the very spot

      where I'd left my stuff

          (even you wouldn't have predicted it):

and now I feel much
like my phone, which lies

drying beside
me in a tub of rice.

SMALL ACTS

She knows something, who can lose herself
in work not of her choosing: who watches
the blown birds wheeling in the kitchen floor,
which is the sky now, she's scrubbed it that hard.

And the undertaker knows, who gives hours
to shinying up his car: it disappears him, and the long sides
rehearse road, church, churchyard, and all the breathing
spaces around them.

And the warden knows, who scales the tower's
steep stone steps each month to polish the bells,
though no one sees them. And the bells of St Andrew's
ring out today. *Observe, observe.*

OF AN HONEST CHURCHGOING MAN QUESTIONED BY A MINISTER ON HIS DEATHBED

And being demanded what he thought of God
he answers that he was a good old man

and what of Christ
that he was a towardly young youth

and of his soul
that it was a great bone in his body

and what should become of his soul after he was dead
that if he had done well he should be put into a pleasant green meadow

THERE HAVE BEEN MOVEMENTS

and still we anticipate the ball
for our entire last year

my vixen
caressing her silken purple gloves

your wolf
hind-legging in a borrowed tuxedo

and trot through the atavistic dances
hoping to be saved the unspeakable

bother of striding
alone across unploughed terrain

which would ruin the shoes we've selected
precisely to inhibit our running away

from the proud deprived mothers
who drop us at the entrance and smile

through tears while their cameras
gobble us up

AT BAY

I try to resist the sway of things I've seen –
images slapping the shore of the brain like

all these jellyfish. I came here to get in,
but no amount of thought can cancel them –

no words, though I tell myself *be brave*;
no numbers, though I count eleven fewer

in the sea to sting me, and know I can bear
much more than a brush with common nettles –

none of it adds up to the pulsing of one
just there, a clump of translucent matter

drifting with no more intention than a weed…

Override, override, but the mind overrides its
self – pale body, water, dread. I back away,

get dressed, drive further up the coast
to try again, a little less intrepid.

THAT SORT OF NOTE

We need more inner red, my friend said.
Show us your inner red.
                                    – Oh, but
my eyes are a hazel branch snapped in two
and my body's a hollow the wind blows through
and the blood in my veins is Polar Sea blue
and –
        The word's denial, my friend said.

PEG,

you're in my dream again
except I'm not asleep

just gazing into the dark house
as you emerge, slim, nose first,

glossy stare fixed. You wait
for me to decide your next move.

I saw your reflection trembling in the window
when fireworks flashed up over the common.

I saw you lurch
at an undefended kitten.

That night I couldn't sleep,
afraid you'd come in.

You're far off now. The door's closed.
It makes no difference.

BLUEBOTTLE

on the carpet under the chair,
with your legs in the air,
how did we come to this *impasse?*

To pinch you by a wing
—a pliant or a
brittle wing—
to expel
you would implicate me
in that which no body
can understand.

And so
I lie down. Let the gauze be drawn
over our simple / compound eyes.

SHOULD ANYONE BE LEFT ALIVE

Sea flows in
        over the sill of a
                square hole (glass long

gone) recarpets
        the carpet (water
                and weed) (shell and

samphire) swells
        the wallpaper (a circle
                of ferns) (a cluster of dandelions

steadfast on a
        bank) ruffles the curtains
                which hang on and stir at

the slightest
        exhalation (unbrushed
                hair around a secret face)

Should anyone
        be left alive where
                would they sit (the sofa

sodden) (the
        level risen well
                beyond their knees)

DAFFODILS PUSH THROUGH IN THE MILD FIRST DAYS OF JANUARY,

prompting my colleague to say 'too soon –
they'll regret it next week when a hard frost sets in'.

And yet, for them, *early* and *late* don't mean;
they do what they do while conditions allow; and if to him

they symbolise disappointment or failure,
or the hubris of the eager,

they also show how nature deals not in *ought*
but *is* – the blip of green or yellow breaking up black

soil, perhaps not making it.

DISAPPEARING ACT

How could I say
I'm sorry?

Evasion confounds
me also.

Sometimes I look
into transparency

as though air
remakes my body;

as an ocean
nurtures lakes

within its depths.
I knew you'd sensed

a ripple
out of the corner of your eye:

something wrong
though nothing

you could place
a finger on.

I fear one day
I'll do great

mischief
without intending to.

THE ENTANGLED BANK

'these elaborately constructed forms, so different from each other, and dependent on each other in so complex a manner'
– Charles Darwin

Diverged
we've no end of innovations

methods for survival
you name them

yet cannot grow
out of the pattern

roots   faces
pulling down   swivelling up

can't not strive
for the sun's approval

are diminished
when she turns away

GLOUCESTER, MASSACHUSETTS was inspired by two
details in Sebastian Junger's book *The Perfect Storm* (1997),
which narrates the events surrounding the disappearance of
the *Andrea Gail* and her crew in October 1991.

OH, SUSIE, IT IS DANGEROUS takes its title from a letter
of Emily Dickinson's to Susan Gilbert, written in early June
1852 and sometimes referred to as 'the marriage letter'.

IN THE POET'S BEDROOM references Emily Dickinson's
Homestead (now a museum and writers' residence) in
Amherst, Massachusetts.

OF AN HONEST CHURCHGOING MAN QUESTIONED
BY A MINISTER ON HIS DEATHBED is an arrangement
of an anecdote related in *The workes of that learned minister
of Gods holy Word, Mr. William Pemble*, 3rd edition (London,
1635), p. 559.

ACKNOWLEDGEMENTS

Versions of some of these poems previously appeared in the following publications: *Ambit, Bath Magg, The Fenland Reed, The Forward Book of Poetry 2020, The Literateur, Live Canon 2019 Anthology,* the London Review Bookshop blog, *The North, PN Review, Poetry Ireland Review, St John's College Poetry Pamphlet* (2018), *The Scores, The Spectator, Taking Note: Poetry in Moments* (2018) and the *TLS*.

'Amnesiac' was commissioned by Helen Napper to accompany her 2016 exhibition 'The Art of Sea Swimming'.

'Notations for a Hospital', 'Corridor', 'Admission' and 'When all this is over' were commissioned by Addenbrooke's Arts and Cambridge Curiosity and Imagination as part of their 2017 'Taking Note' project at Addenbrooke's Hospital.

I am indebted to the Hawthornden Literary Retreat for a Fellowship in 2019.

Huge thanks to Sarah Hall, Penny Boxall and Adam Crothers for their encouragement, detailed edits and significant help in shaping the collection. Thanks also to Michael Schmidt, Charlotte Rowland, Alan Jenkins, James Richards and everyone in the Panton workshop group for notes on individual poems, and to Jacob Polley for looking through the draft typescript.

The title poem is dedicated to Sarah, along with several other poems inspired by our chats and adventures.

'Music in Four Parts', which remembers the musician and composer Fergal O'Mahony (1983–2014), is for James.